The 2000s

Britain in Pictures

AMMONITE
PRESS

PRESS
ASSOCIATION
Images

First Published 2010 by
Ammonite Press
an imprint of AE Publications Ltd,
166 High Street, Lewes, East Sussex, BN7 1XU

Text © AE Publications Ltd
Images © Press Association Images
© Copyright in the Work AE Publications Ltd

ISBN 978-1-906672-57-7

British Cataloguing in Publication Data. A catalogue
record of this book is available from the British Library.

Editor: Ian Penberthy
Series Editor: Richard Wiles
Picture research: Press Association Images
Design: Gravemaker + Scott

Colour reproduction by GMC Reprographics
Printed and bound in China by Hung Hing Off-Set

Page 2: Manchester United's Cristiano Ronaldo (L) celebrates with Rio Ferdinand (R) and the rest of the team after beating Chelsea for the Champions League trophy. The match was drawn 1–1, but United won on penalties, 6–5.
21st May, 2008

Page 5: Queen Elizabeth II smiles at the Duke of Edinburgh on Horseguards Parade during the annual Trooping of the Colour.
13th June, 2009

Page 6: In the aftermath of the terrorist attack on the twin towers of the World Trade Center in Manhattan, New York, fire crews and other emergency personnel regroup against a backdrop of twisted steelwork.
12th September, 2001

Introduction

The archives of PA Photos yield a unique insight into Britain's recent past. Thanks to the science of photography, we can view the past 150 years or so more accurately than any period that came before, but it is thanks to news photography, and in particular the great news agency that is The Press Association, that we are able now to witness the events that made up life in Britain not so long ago.

It is easy, looking back, to imagine the past neatly partitioned into clearly defined periods and dominated by milestones: wars, political upheaval and economic trends. But the archives tell a different story: alongside the major events that constitute formal history are found the smaller things that had equal – if not greater – significance for ordinary people at the time. And while the photographers were working for that moment's news rather than posterity, the camera is indiscriminate, recording everything in its view: to modern eyes, it is often the backgrounds of these pictures, not their intended subjects, that provide the greatest fascination. Likewise, we see that Britain does not pass neatly from one period to another.

As the debris of the New Year's revels was swept away, people awoke on 1st January, 2000 to the dawn of not only a new year, but also a new decade, a new century and a new millennium. The feared 'Y2K Bug' had failed to have serious detrimental impact on the world's computer systems when the clocks rolled over to the year 2000. Reason indeed to adopt a spirit of optimism. That optimistic outlook would be needed, however, for the events of the new decade would be challenging for many.

It would seem as though the bad news simply wouldn't stop coming: widespread foot-and-mouth disease decimating the country's livestock; race riots; the devastating attack on the World Trade Center in New York, which had far-reaching effects in Britain and throughout the world; the deaths of Princess Margaret and the Queen Mother; terrorist bombings on London's public transport systems and at Glasgow airport; the banking system in crisis; flooding and other extreme weather events said to be caused by global warming; the scandal of MP's expenses; the MMR jab and swine flu scares. And underpinning it all, the controversial War on Terror in Afghanistan and Iraq, which led to the deaths of many British servicemen and women, a war that still raged as the first decade of the 21st century came to an end.

Britons needed the indomitability and stoicism of earlier generations, who had weathered the storms of two world wars and the Depression of the 1930s. And they found that spirit when it came to celebrating Queen Elizabeth II's Golden Jubilee, and in savouring the success of British athletes at the Olympic Games of 2000, 2004 and 2008, and in many other sporting endeavours at home and abroad.

Twenty-first century life in the British Isles, as it turned out, was not all a tale of doom and gloom. There were many reasons to be cheerful, and in the words of a famous wartime poster, to keep calm and carry on.

One is not terribly amused. Clearly unused to the familiarity, a reluctant Queen Elizabeth holds hands with Prime Minister Tony Blair and his wife, Cherie, as the crowd sings *Auld Lang Syne* during midnight celebrations to welcome in the New Year at the Millennium Dome.

1st January, 2000

The **2000s** Britain in Pictures

At the stroke of midnight, fireworks explode over one of London's most recognizable landmarks, the clock tower that stands at the north end of the Palace of Westminster, as the chimes of Big Ben, the bell it houses, resound, ushering in not only a new year, but also a new millennium in the United Kingdom.

1st January, 2000

Revellers greet the dramatic dawn of a new millennium from the hill on which stands the 'Angel of the North' in Gateshead. The construction of Antony Gormley's 66ft (20m) tall steel sculpture, with its 178ft (54m) wingspan, initially courted controversy, but the landmark has since been widely accepted as an icon for the north-east of England.

1st January, 2000

Facing page: Dealers at work in the dealing room at the Royal Bank of Scotland in Holborn, London. The Millennium Bug, or Y2K, failed to make the predicted disastrous impact upon computer systems when the clocks rolled over into the year 2000. In computer programs, the practice of representing the year with two digits caused some date-related processing to operate incorrectly, but the global 'meltdown' of computer systems failed to materialize.

4th January, 2000

Facing page: The Guizer Jarl and his squad, drawn from Shetlanders dressed in Viking costume, set fire to the Galley, a 30ft (9m) replica wooden longship, which they have dragged in a torchlit procession through the streets of Lerwick in the Shetland Isles. The festival of Up Helly Aa, although based on Norse pagan celebrations of feasting and fires, originated in the 1880s to celebrate the end of the yule season.
25th January, 2000

Sinn Féin President Gerry Adams with Martin McGuinness speaking to the press at Parliament buildings in Belfast on the day Secretary of State for Northern Ireland Peter Mandelson suspended the Northern Ireland Assembly, following reports from the International Commission on Decommissioning that it had "*received no information from the IRA as to when decommissioning will start*".
11th February, 2000

Spice Girl Victoria Beckham, also known as 'Posh Spice', makes her debut on the catwalk with a guest appearance in designer Maria Grachvogel's Autumn/Winter Collection 2000 show at the National History Museum, as part of London Fashion Week.

16th February, 2000

Tickling stick. An anti-capitalism demonstrator, dressed in a carnival fairy costume, taunts riot police with a feather duster in Trafalgar Square, central London during a march from Parliament Square.
1st May, 2000

The statue of Sir Winston Churchill was defaced with graffiti and a turf 'mohican' attached to its head during the May Day anti-capitalism demonstration in Parliament Square, where 'Guerrilla Gardeners' planted trees and plants in piles of manure.
1st May, 2000

Self-made men. Entrepreneurs Amstrad chairman Alan Sugar (L), Virgin boss Richard Branson (second R), and EasyJet chairman Stelios Haji-Iannou (R) joke with Prime Minister Tony Blair at the launch in Downing Street of Enterprise Insight, a new business initiative to provide *"insight and consulting services to Chief Information Officers (CIOs) and the Information Technology marketplace in areas of market research and consulting, moderation and facilitation of executive thought leadership events, presentations and briefings."*
11th May, 2000

Facing page: Glastonbury Festival organizer Michael Eavis, resplendent in dinner jacket, whisks Marielle Troup around the dance floor as ballroom dancing is featured in the Somerset music festival, on the first day of the three-day annual event.
23rd June, 2000

At the launch of a project to improve grassroots football skills, England manager Kevin Keegan heads a ball as Prime Minister Tony Blair watches in the back garden of 10 Downing Street, London. The new Football Foundation will encourage youngsters into the sport and improve facilities with millions of pounds raised through the sale of Premiership television rights. The launch comes as Culture Secretary Chris Smith is due to announce to the Commons details of the Government's increased spending on sport.
25th July, 2000

The Queen Mother celebrates her 100th birthday from the balcony of Buckingham Palace with her daughter, Queen Elizabeth II. Thousands of people flocked to the streets to cheer the longest living Royal in the history of the monarchy.
4th August, 2000

Eleven-year-old actor Daniel Radcliffe (C), who is to play the title role in the forthcoming film *Harry Potter and the Sorcerer's Stone*, based on the book by J.K. Rowling, with co-stars Rupert Grint (Ron Weasley) and Emma Watson (Hermione Granger) at the Berkeley Hotel in London.

23rd August, 2000

Metropolitan Police Commissioner Sir John Stevens launches a year-long series of initiatives to raise £5m to establish a crime fighting institute in memory of murdered television presenter Jill Dando at New Scotland Yard in London. BBC Crimewatch presenter Dando, 37, had been shot dead in April 1999 on the steps of her home in Fulham, west London. Her death sparked a police manhunt that led to the controversial conviction, retrial and, in 2008, acquittal of Barry George.
12th September, 2000

Great Britain's rowers (L–R) Matthew Pinsent, Steve Redgrave and James Cracknell, along with Tim Foster (not pictured), celebrate after winning the gold medal in the Men's Coxless Four final at the Olympic Games held in Sydney, Australia.
23rd September, 2000

Great Britain's Denise Lewis celebrates winning the gold medal in the Women's Heptathlon at the Olympic Games in Sydney. Lewis was awarded an OBE for services to athletics in the Queen's New Year's Honours list.

24th September, 2000

Facing page: Workers cheer as the 5,387,862nd and final classic Mini rolls off the production line at the MG Rover Group factory in Longbridge, Birmingham. After 41 years of continuous production and nearly 140 different models, one of Britain's best-loved cars is being superseded by a new version made by German car giant BMW, which will be produced at the Cowley works in Oxford.

4th October, 2000

1959-2000

Waves crash against the promenade in Dover after parts of Britain were lashed by a massive overnight storm that claimed at least two lives. The severe weather caused millions of pounds of damage, and plunged road and rail networks into chaos. People were warned to stay at home as emergency services battled to deal with the aftermath of the worst weather to hit the south of England since the great hurricane of 1987.
30th October, 2000

Heads up! Aston Villa captain Gareth Southgate (L) leads
the charge for a loose ball during the team's FA Premiership
match against Everton at their home ground in Goodison
Park, Liverpool.
5th November, 2000

A cleaner vacuums around Morag the sheep at the Royal Museum in Edinburgh, Scotland. Morag was the first sheep to be cloned from differentiated cells by the Roslin Institute, which had donated the preserved animal to the museum. Scientists had cloned Morag and her twin sister, Megan, from embryo cells in a laboratory in 1995, an achievement that later led to the creation of Dolly the sheep, the first mammal to be cloned from an adult somatic cell.
17th November, 2000

The world's largest floating crane, Asian Hercules II, lifts the 850-tonne Gateshead Millennium Bridge into its permanent position spanning the River Tyne. The £22m bridge had been designed to create a pedestrian and cycling link between the Gateshead Quays and the neighbouring Newcastle quayside. The bridge rotates to allow boats to pass underneath, the movement having been likened to the blinking of an eye.

20th November, 2000

Agatha Christie's famous whodunit, *The Mousetrap*, was due to celebrate its 20,000th performance on 16th December, 2000 at the St Martins Theatre in London's West End, during its 49th year. Listed in Guinness World Records as the world's longest running play, *The Mousetrap* opened at London's Ambassador Theatre on 25th November, 1952.
7th December, 2000

Crowned head. Harrods chairman Mohamed Al Fayed dons a Victorian emerald and diamond tiara, reduced from £78,000 to £58,500, after Welsh singer Charlotte Church had inaugurated the Knightsbridge store's January sale in London.
3rd January, 2001

A great plume of acrid smoke rises into the blue wintry sky from a pit on Netherplace Farm, Lockerbie in Scotland, where all the cattle and sheep were being burned. The farm was the first in Scotland to be affected by the outbreak of foot-and-mouth disease.
4th March, 2001

England's Man of the Series,
Darren Gough, is thrown in
the air by his team mates,
using a flag of St George,
as they celebrate the Third
Test victory over Sri Lanka,
in Colombo.
17th March, 2001

Deputy Prime Minister John Prescott and Craig Evans scuffle on the ground after the latter had thrown an egg at the politician, who had responded by punching him. The fracas occurred after Prescott was surrounded by protesters when he arrived to address a Labour Party rally at Rhyl's Little Theatre, North Wales during the General Election campaign. After investigating the incident, the Crown Prosecution Service decided not to press charges against either Prescott or Evans.
16th May, 2001

Ian Paisley, leader of the Democratic Unionist Party, gives the thumbs-up as he arrives at a polling station in his native town of Ballymena, north Antrim to vote in the General Election, in which 18 seats are being contested across the province of Northern Ireland.

7th June, 2001

Smoke billows from a burning barricade on Abbey Street in Bradford as members of the Asian community and police continue to clash after a day of violence in the city. Rioting had broken out following racial tension between the area's ethnic minorities and the white majority.

7th July, 2001

Facing page: Sir Thomas Lipton's famous J-class yacht *Shamrock V* pounds through heavy seas in the Solent, off Cowes, Isle of Wight on the first day of racing at the America's Cup Jubilee Regatta.

19 August, 2001

Whistle blowers. Policemen join in the fun at the Notting Hill Carnival in west London. The cost of policing the 2001 street party shot to a record £4m following the violence that had marred the previous year's event, but far fewer arrests were made compared to that year.

27th August, 2001

Ecstatic England fans celebrate victory over Germany in the qualification match for the 2002 World Cup, held at the Olympiastadion, Munich. England's 5–1 victory was aided by a hat trick from Michael Owen.

1st September, 2001

Facing page: Dense smoke from fires burning within the twin towers of New York's World Trade Center stains the sky. Al-Qaeda terrorists had crashed two hijacked airliners into the buildings, both of which would collapse, killing thousands, including many Britons. Another plane had been seized and flown into the Pentagon in Washington, while a fourth, possibly headed towards the White House, had crashed after passengers had fought back against the hijackers.
11th September, 2001

A fire truck ploughs through a cloud of thick dust in the immediate aftermath of the destruction of the World Trade Center in New York. Rescue workers would face an enormous task in recovering the bodies of those killed in the attacks on the twin towers and the Pentagon in Washington.
12th September, 2001

US servicemen carry out an intensive search of every vehicle entering the USAF base at RAF Mildenhall, Suffolk, in a heightening of security after the terrorist attacks in New York and Washington.
15th September, 2001

The Stars and Stripes flies defiantly from the buckled remains of the World Trade Center. The heart of New York's financial district had been destroyed in the terrorist attack, which killed over 5,000 people.
23rd September, 2001

Chicken crossing. Psychologist Dr Richard Wiseman watches student Peter Costello, 17, dressed as a chicken cross the road at the British Association's Festival of Science at Glasgow University. Wiseman was launching The Laugh Lab, a year-long, internet-based study to find the nation's funniest joke and explore the psychology of humour.

September, 2001

Facing page: England's David Beckham celebrates with team mate Emile Heskey after scoring the equalizer from a free kick against Greece during the dying seconds of the FIFA World Cup European Qualifying Group Nine match at the Old Trafford ground, Manchester.

6th October, 2001

British Prime Minister Tony Blair addresses the troops at Al Sha'afa camp in north Oman during a two-day diplomatic visit to the area.
10th October, 2001

Facing page: Protesters on their way to Trafalgar Square from London's Hyde Park, as the march organized by CND against military strikes on Afghanistan gets under way. The assault on Afghanistan had been prompted by the Al-Qaeda attacks on New York and Washington: the terrorist group operated training camps in the country with the connivance of the ruling Taliban.
13th October, 2001

Royal Marines from 40 Commando huddle together with their
equipment as the Royal Navy Sea King helicopter that flew
them in takes off. The Marines were taking part in Exercise
Saif Sarrea in Oman. With conflict in Afghanistan and
increasing belligerence toward Iraq, Britain's forces were on
an urgent training schedule in the Middle East.
19th October, 2001

British Prime Minister Tony Blair is greeted by Sayed Abdu
Majid Al-Khoei (second R), head of the Shia muslims in the
United Kingdom, and Sheikh Dr M.A. Zaki Badawi (L) and
Sheikh Fadhel Sahlani (R), from the New York Al-Khoei
Foundation, as he arrives at the Al-Khoei Foundation in
north-west London, where he would give an address to an
Islamic conference.
25th October, 2001

Kylie Minogue performing on stage during the Smash Hits T4 Poll Winners Party at the London Arena in Docklands. She would be voted the world's sexiest star, taking the title ahead of such celebrities as Catherine Zeta-Jones, Britney Spears and Nicole Kidman.
9th December, 2001

Cherie Blair, wife of British Prime Minister Tony Blair, meets local people during a visit to the village of Vattem in Andhar Pradesh, India, where she and her husband saw British funded education and water projects.
6th January, 2002

Facing page: The Royal Navy's 16,000-ton nuclear submarine HMS *Vanguard*. Equipped with Trident ballistic missiles, she was launched in March 1992 and is based at Faslane on the Clyde. In February 2002, she would undergo a two-year refit at Devonport, Plymouth, during which time she was boarded illegally by two anti-nuclear protesters.
3rd January, 2002

Prime Minister Tony Blair and the interim leader of Afghanistan, Hamid Karzai, during a press conference in Downing Street, London. Karzai would be elected president in 2004, and again in 2009 after his opponent withdrew.
3rd January, 2002

Wave power. Trams on
Blackpool seafront had to
be towed to safety after high
tides and gale-force winds
battered the coastline.
1st February, 2002

The final two contestants in the first series of the television talent show *Pop Idol*, Gareth Gates (L) and Will Young, face to face at a photocall in Stephen Street, London, following the voting off of Darius Danesh. Young would go on to win and develop a successful pop career. Gates would also become a professional singer, but would concentrate his efforts on stage musicals.
3rd February, 2002

Oasis front man Liam Gallagher performs on stage at the Royal Albert Hall, London, during a fundraising concert in aid of the Teenage Cancer Trust.
6th February, 2002

Facing page: Two military knights maintain a vigil at the coffin of Princess Margaret before her funeral in St George's Chapel, Windsor Castle. Some 400 family, friends and staff were expected at the service. Princess Margaret, the younger sister of Queen Elizabeth II, had died on 9th February, 2002, aged 71.
15th February, 2002

A smiling Jim Broadbent shows off his Best Supporting Actor award for the film *Iris* at the 74th Annual Academy Awards (Oscars) at the Kodak Theater in Hollywood. The film was a biographical account of novelist Iris Murdoch's relationship with John Bayley. Broadbent co-starred with Judi Dench and Kate Winslet.

24th March, 2002

The coffin of Queen
Elizabeth, the Queen Mother
is carried into Westminster
Hall, where she will lie in
state until her funeral at
Westminster Abbey. She had
died on 20th March, 2002, at
the great age of 101.
5th April, 2002

The coffin of Queen Elizabeth, the Queen Mother is placed on the catafalque in Westminster Abbey during her funeral service. It is estimated that more than a million people filled the area outside the Abbey and lined the route to her final resting place at St George's Chapel, Windsor Castle.

9th April, 2002

Flora London Marathon participant LLoyd Scott, from
Rainham in Essex, takes a break for lunch in Goddards
Pie and Mash House, Greenwich. Scott was walking
the London Marathon in full diving gear for the CLIC
(Cancer and Leukaemia in Childhood) charity, based
in Bristol. A survivor of leukaemia, Scott has raised more
than £4m for cancer charities.
15th April, 2002

Part of a train is wedged beneath the platform canopy after
a high-speed rail crash at Potter's Bar station, Hertfordshire.
The accident, caused by faulty points, killed seven and
injured 76. Railtrack, responsible for maintenance of
the track, said it was not aware that there had been any
indication of problems on that particular stretch of track.
The company's comment came after reports that both
passengers and drivers had felt a bump when trains crossed
the accident point.
11th May, 2002

Facing page: A street party
in the Village area of south
Belfast to celebrate Queen
Elizabeth II's Golden Jubilee.
Similar events were held
throughout the nation.
1st June, 2002

First birds, now frogs.
Heavy metal singer Ozzy
Osbourne, notorious for
having bitten the head off a
dove while intoxicated, hams
it up with Kermit the Frog
backstage in the gardens
of Buckingham Palace
during the second concert
to commemorate the Golden
Jubilee of Queen Elizabeth
II. Some 12,000 tickets were
distributed by ballot for the
Party at the Palace, and tens
of thousands more gathered
outside to enjoy the music.
3rd June, 2002

Projected images record the 50-year reign of Queen
Elizabeth II on the facade of Buckingham Palace in London
after the Party at the Palace, the second concert to be held
in the grounds in three days.
3rd June, 2002

Queen Elizabeth II and the Duke of Edinburgh wave to the crowds as they are driven in the Gold State Coach from Buckingham Palace to St Paul's Cathedral for a service of thanksgiving to celebrate her Golden Jubilee.
4th June, 2002

A member of the US special forces stands with a British Royal Marine outside the mud-brick barn in Atalay village, 50 miles (80km) north-west of Kandahar in southern Afghanistan, where they discovered a cache of weapons and explosives. The British and American forces faced an uphill struggle to oust the Taliban regime and prevent the country from continuing as a breeding ground for terrorism, a struggle that continues to this day.
6th June, 2002

Lennox Lewis holds the belts for his three retained heavyweight titles (WBC, IBF and IBO) after he knocked out the former champion, Mike Tyson, in the eighth round at the Pyramid Arena, Memphis, USA.
9th June, 2002

Facing page: England's goalkeeper, David Seaman, can only watch as he is beaten by Brazil's Ronaldinho from a free kick. The goal gave Brazil the victory.
21st June, 2002

Sunshine instead of the traditional rain caused Emma
Harris, 31, from London, to don her sunglasses during the
Glastonbury Festival 2002, in Pilton, Somerset.
29th June, 2002

Where's me didgeridoo, blue? In front of a crowd of adoring fans, evergreen Rolf Harris performs on the main stage at the Glastonbury music festival in Pilton, Somerset. He had made his debut at the festival in 1994 and subsequently was named the best entertainer ever to have appeared there.
30th June, 2002

The Beinn An Tuirc wind farm on the Kintyre peninsula in Scotland. The giant propellers continue to be controversial and face opposition in many areas, but wind farms are a major aspect of Britain's programme to generate electricity from renewable sources. One of the arguments against them is that they can have a detrimental effect on military and radar installations.
8th July, 2002

Facing page: England's football captain, David Beckham, and Kirsty Howard hand the Queen's Jubilee Baton to Queen Elizabeth II after its final leg around the City of Manchester Stadium, during the opening ceremony of the Commonwealth Games.
25th July, 2002

Jade Goody, a contestant in the Channel 4 reality TV show *Big Brother*, is interviewed on the big screen after being evicted from the Big Brother House. Goody's time in the house would make her a celebrity, and she would return for the celebrity version of the show in 2007, when she was accused of racist bullying. For a while she would be reviled in the press, but the onset of cervical cancer would see her return to the public eye. She would die from cancer on 22nd March, 2009.

26th July, 2002

Flowers left by the public in the graveyard of St Andrew's Church, Soham, in Cambridgeshire, in memory of Holly Wells and Jessica Chapman. The two 10-year-old girls had been murdered by 28-year-old school caretaker Ian Huntley.

26th August, 2002

European Ryder Cup captain Sam Torrance holds the Ryder Cup on the 10th green bridge, at the Belfry, near Sutton Coldfield in Warwickshire. The European team had won the cup by a margin of 15½ to 12½. The event had been postponed from September 2001 as a result of the attack on the World Trade Center in New York, and thereafter Ryder Cup matches were held in even-numbered years.

30th September, 2002

A Friends of the Earth protester, dressed as the devil, hands out leaflets to passers-by outside Esso's London headquarters, as a protest against Esso's stance on climate change. Friends of the Earth claimed that Esso had been lobbying against international action to tackle global warming.
31st October, 2002

A worker lifts a salmon at a fish farm on Loch Linnhe, near Fort William, on the west coast of Scotland. Outbreaks of sea lice, together with accusations that farmed salmon were artificially coloured, and could contain PCBs (Polychlorinated biphenyls) and dioxins, had put the fish farming industry under severe pressure.

3rd November, 2002

Celebrity chef Jamie Oliver at work in the kitchen during the launch of his new restaurant, Fifteen, in London's Old Street. The restaurant is staffed by professional chefs and 15 unemployed young people, who have been given the opportunity to work in the kitchens as part of a training programme. All profits from the restaurant will go to Cheeky Chops, a charity set up by Oliver to support the additional training of current and future students.
7th November, 2002

Detective Chief Inspector Dick Harrison outside Northampton Crown Court with a knife allegedly used by four men to kill 17-year-old Ross Parker in Peterborough in September 2001. The court was told that Shaied Nazir, 21, Ziaraff Mahrad, 21, Ahmed Ali Awan, 22, and Sarfraz Ali, 25, had murdered the teenager in front of his girlfriend. Mahrad was cleared, but the other three received life sentences.

7th November, 2002

Facing page: A taxi turns off Park Lane in central London, passing over road markings that indicate the location of the congestion charging zone that was due to become operational on 17th February, 2003. Motorists would be charged £5 per day for driving within the zone, from 7am to 6.30pm, Monday to Friday.

31st December, 2002

Wembley Stadium's famous twin towers are all that remain of the structure in west London, which had been demolished to make way for a new facility. The towers would also soon be knocked down, the process being started by Ray Tidmarsh, from Dawlish in Devon, who had won the right in a radio competition. When completed, the new Wembley Stadium would be the largest football stadium in the world, with every seat under cover and no restricted views. The arch – with a span of 1,033ft (315m) – would be the longest single-span roof structure in the world.

6th February, 2003

British boxer Audley Harrison delivers a punishing blow to Rob Calloway's jaw. Harrison would go on to beat the American in four rounds.
8th February, 2003

Singer Ms Dynamite
performing on stage during
The Brit Awards 2003 at
Earls Court 2, London. She
would receive the British
female solo artist and best
British urban act awards.
20th February, 2003

Voice from the past. Veteran DJ, Tony Blackburn (L), whose voice was the first ever to be heard on Radio 1, in 1967, joins Chris Moyles at Yalding House in London for his daily show. Blackburn had left the BBC in 1984.

10th March, 2003

Fashion designer Zandra Rhodes with fashion and portrait photographer Rankin at the Re:creation Awards for young creative talent at the Victoria and Albert Museum, in London. Known for her brightly coloured hair, and extravagant make-up and clothes, Rhodes had been one of a group of new designers who had put London at the forefront of the international fashion scene in the 1970s.
19th March, 2003

Curled into a ball for protection, jockey Robert 'Choc' Thornton waits for the field to pass after falling from Windross during the Martell Cognac V.S. Thresher handicap steeple chase at Aintree Racecourse, Liverpool.
4th April, 2003

Abu Hamza al-Masri addresses an audience of more than 100 Muslims during lunchtime prayers outside Finsbury Park Mosque, north London. In October 2004, the radical Islamist would be arrested and charged with a number of crimes, including encouraging the murder of non-Muslims and inciting racial hatred. He would be jailed for seven years, after which he would face extradition to the USA, where he had been charged with attempting to set up a terrorist training camp.

11th April, 2003

Wigan's Martin Aspinwall (L) is held back by Bradford's Lee Radford during their Powergen semi-final at the Alfred McAlpine Stadium, Huddersfield. Bradford would go on to win the match 36–22.

13th April, 2003

Thousands of holidaymakers
flock to the beach at
Bournemouth in Dorset, as
temperatures soar into the
30s on one of the hottest
days of the year so far.
15th July, 2003

The British nuclear submarine HMS *Splendid* (L) travels
in the company of three sister vessels, HMS *Sovereign*
(second L), HMS *Sceptre* and HMS *Spartan* (R), near Arran
on the west coast of Scotland. All are of the Swiftsure class,
designed originally to be armed with torpedoes, mines and
anti-ship missiles.
17th July, 2003

Facing page: A soldier from the Queen's Lancashire Regiment warily checks a bombed building in Basra, Iraq. British forces had been training local Iraqis, many of whom had belonged to Saddam Hussein's vast army before the war, to become the country's new police force, in the hope that this would soon allow them to leave the country.
24th September, 2003

Supermodel Naomi Campbell wears a creation from Jasper Conran's Spring/Summer 2004 collection, during London Fashion Week at the Duke of York's Headquarters in Central London.
24th September, 2003

A patrol from the King's Own Scottish Borderers encounters a camel train near the Tigris River, outside Al Amara in Northern Iraq. One of the most important tasks of the British troops in the country was to win over the local populace.
27th September, 2003

Catch of the day. Celebrity chef Gordon Ramsay, surrounded by catering students from Lewisham College, holds up a 64lb (29kg) halibut during a photocall to launch National Seafood Week at Billingsgate Fish Market in east London.
2nd October, 2003

Two men, dwarfed by the vast Turbine Hall inside the Tate Modern gallery on London's South Bank, experience Olafur Eliasson's installation entitled 'The Weather Project'. Eliasson had installed humidifiers to create a fine mist, while a huge sun-like structure, made of hundreds of monochromatic lamps, radiated a yellow light.
15th October, 2003

End of an era. Captain Mike Bannister (R) and Senior First Officer Jonathan Napier wave from the cockpit of a British Airways Concorde at London's Heathrow Airport, on the day that the world's first supersonic airliner retired from commercial service. Thousands of people gathered at the airport to see three of the aircraft land one after the other.
24th October, 2003

Prime Minister Tony Blair and US President George
W. Bush return to 10 Downing Street, London, after
giving a press conference at the Foreign Office. Both
men had sent armies to invade Iraq in March because
of Saddam Hussein's refusal to give up the weapons
of mass destruction they claimed he possessed. In
fact, no such weapons existed.
19th November, 2003

Facing page: Queen Elizabeth II arrives with
President George W. Bush at a Buckingham Palace
banquet in honour of the president, during the first
day of his four-day state visit to the UK.
19th November, 2003

With the score standing at 17–17, Jonny Wilkinson kicks the winning goal to clinch the Rugby World Cup for England in the last minute of extra time of a thrilling final with Australia at Telstra Stadium in Sydney.

22nd November, 2003

Facing page: England captain Martin Johnson holds the Webb Ellis trophy aloft after his team beat Australia in the Rugby World Cup final in Sydney, Australia.

22nd November, 2003

Britain's enigmatic former Prime Minister Baroness Thatcher sits alone as she waits for the start of the State Opening of Parliament at the Palace of Westminster in London.
26th November, 2003

Facing page: Proud England football captain David Beckham kisses his wife, ex-Spice Girl Victoria, after being awarded the OBE (Officer of the Order of the British Empire) by The Queen at Buckingham Palace, London.
27th November, 2003

Sweet sensation. Nigella Lawson makes a special appearance alongside a life-size chocolate sculpture of the celebrity cook, part of the Christmas window displays at Selfridges, Oxford Street, central London.
6th December, 2003

Television personality Jonathan Ross celebrates the award for Best Comedy Entertainment Programme, given to him for *Friday Night With Jonathan Ross* during the annual British Comedy Awards at London Television Studios in south London.
10th December, 2003

Professor Colin Pillinger, chief scientist of the Beagle 2 Mars lander project, during a press conference given after his team had failed to receive a signal from the lander telling them that it had safely reached the surface of the planet. Despite several attempts to communicate with the probe, no contact was made and its fate remains a mystery.

25th December, 2003

A large crowd welcomes the world's biggest and most expensive cruise liner, Cunard's *Queen Mary 2*, as she arrives at her new home port of Southampton. The £550m ship would be officially named at Southampton by the Queen on 8th January; four days later, the 150,000-tonne vessel would leave on her sold-out maiden passenger voyage to Fort Lauderdale, Florida.

26th December, 2003

Outside the Purple Haze Café in Edinburgh, police officers hand out guidelines on the use of cannabis after it was downgraded to a Class-C drug. The café, a private members' club, would not sell cannabis, but members would be able to smoke it on the premises.

29th January, 2004

Former binman Michael Carroll, self proclaimed 'King of Chavs', who won £9.7m on the national Lottery in 2002, arrives at Swaffham Magistrates Court in Norfolk for sentencing. Three weeks before, Carroll, 20, of Swaffham had admitted possessing 0.7oz (19.7g) of cocaine plus a number of other drugs offences. By 2006 it was reported that Carroll was almost broke, having spent his fortune on new homes, drugs, parties, gold jewellery, prostitutes and cars.

2nd March, 2004

The Prince of Wales and his eldest son, Prince William,
enjoy a joke with the waiting reporters and photographers on
the Madrisa ski slopes, above the Swiss village of Klosters.
28th March, 2004

Comedians (L–R) Matt
Lucas, Ricky Gervais and
David Walliams arrive for
the British Academy of Film
and Television Arts (BAFTA)
Awards at the Grosvenor
House Hotel in Park Lane,
central London.
18th April, 2004

Smile till it hurts. Victoria
and David Beckham arrive
for 19 Management's party
celebrating 19 years in
business, at the Royal Albert
Hall in central London.
19th April, 2004

Glamour model Katie Price (aka Jordan) and her fiancé, Peter Andre. The couple met while appearing on the television show *I'm a Celebrity, Get Me Out of Here*. They would marry on 10th September, 2005, in the refined surroundings of Highclere Castle in Berkshire. Subsequently, they would appear in a long-running, 'fly-on-the-wall' documentary about their lives, and would continue to court the cameras after their divorce in 2009.
4th June, 2004

French children play near a cross and poppy left in the sand on Arromanches beach, Normandy in remembrance of the Allied soldiers who lost their lives while taking part in the D-Day landings on 6th June, 1944. The action was the largest amphibious operation in history, involving 175,000 troops together with over 5,000 ships and their crews.

6th June, 2004

Facing page: The inscription on the Diana, Princess of Wales Memorial Fountain in London's Hyde Park, which was opened officially by Queen Elizabeth II on 6th July, 2004. Designed by American landscape artist Kathryn Gustafson, the fountain was created to evoke the Princess's spirit and love of children. Although described as a fountain, in fact it takes the form of an oval granite rill.

6th July, 2004

Facing page: David Coulthard drives his Mclaren Mercedes Formula One car during a demonstration in the West End of London. The purpose of the event was to show how the city could host its own grand prix, much like the annual race in Monte Carlo, but nothing ever came of the idea.
6th July, 2004

In the wake of several disasters, including the 2004 Madrid train bombing and the 2001 foot-and-mouth epidemic, the British Home Office sent a booklet entitled *Preparing for Emergencies* to every home in the country. The 22-page publication contained a variety of useful advice on coping with natural disasters, accidents and acts of terrorism.
26th July, 2004

Belly flop. Visitors to Brighton beach in Sussex dive off the sea wall to cool off as temperatures soar.
1st August, 2004

Italy's Giancarlo DeMatteis (R) flies through the air after crashing badly and is narrowly missed by Warwick Nowland during the second of the day's races of round eight of the World Superbike Championships at Brands Hatch, Kent. The Italian sustained a broken collarbone and wrist.
1st August, 2004

Emergency services personnel contemplate the devastation caused by a wall of water that tore through the picturesque holiday spot of Boscastle in north Cornwall after torrential rainfall had caused flooding. A massive rescue operation involving several helicopters was put into action to save the residents of the flood-ravaged coastal village.
17th August, 2004

Facing page: Three blondes in a boat. Great Britain's Olympic gold medal winning Yngling sailing crew, (L–R) Shirley Robertson, Sarah Webb and Sarah Ayton leap for joy at their win.
19th August, 2004

Great Britain's gold medal winner Kelly Holmes celebrates winning the 800m during the Olympic Games in Athens, Greece. Holmes would also win gold in the 1,500m, and for her achievements would be made a Dame Commander of the Order of the British Empire (DBE) in the New Year's Honours List of 2005.
23rd August, 2004

American pop singer Madonna performs for Irish fans at Slane Castle, Co Meath, in the Republic of Ireland during her Re-Invention World Tour. The tour was in support of her ninth album, *American Life*.

29th August, 2004

Down and out. England's Michael Vaughan is stumped by Indian wicketkeeper Dinesh Karthik for 74 during the final NatWest Challenge match at Lord's Cricket Ground, London. The three-match challenge was won by England 2–1.

5th September, 2004

First World War veteran Henry Allingham, 108, with a Nieuport biplane at the British Air Services Memorial, which had just been unveiled at St Omer Airfield in France. Allingham was the last survivor of the Battle of Jutland, the last survivor of the Royal Naval Air Service and the last surviving founding member of the Royal Air Force. He died in 2009, having reached the age of 113.

11th September, 2004

Great Britain's Tanni Grey-Thompson waves to her family after finishing the Women's T54 200m final in fourth place at the 2004 Paralympic Games in Athens, Greece. She would gain gold medals in the 100m and 400m events. Born with spina bifida, Grey-Thompson is considered one of the most successful of the UK's disabled athletes.

27th September, 2004

A soldier from 51 Squadron RAF Regiment gives a thumbs-up to two men playing football at the side of the road, on the outskirts of Basra, southern Iraq during an early morning patrol. The RAF Regiment was formed in 1942 to provide airfield defence against ground-based threats so that air operations can continue unhindered.

1st October, 2004

Home Secretary David Blunkett and actress Liz Smith,
star of *The Royle Family* television sitcom, join Second
World War veterans to announce the implementation of
free passports for all British citizens born on or before 2nd
September, 1929, at the Cabinet War Rooms in King Charles
Street, central London.
13th October, 2004

Superdads. Fathers 4 Justice defendants (L–R) Jason Hatch, Dave Pyke, Mark Peacock and Pat Lennon arrive at Weston-super-Mare Magistrates Court, where four supporters look down from the roof. The pressure group for fathers' rights had staged a number of protest stunts, and on 13th September, 2004, Hatch and Pyke had managed to evade Buckingham Palace security and scale the building.
20th October, 2004

The scene of a rail crash in Ufton Nervet, Berkshire, where six people died and 11 were seriously injured. Dozens more were treated for minor cuts and bruises. Many were trapped in the wreckage after the First Great Western service carrying 300 passengers ploughed into a car on an automatic crossing near Reading.

7th November, 2004

An AEC Routemaster bus arrives at Buckingham Palace in London, where it will join other design classics, including a Mini and the nose-cone from a supersonic Concorde, in the quadrangle of the Queen's official residence for an exhibition showcasing British excellence entitled the 'Avenue of Design'.

22nd November, 2004

Former Atomic Kitten singer Jenny Frost (second L) and Breakfast News presenter Natasha Kaplinsky (R) help man telephones at London's BT Tower, taking details of donations made by the public in response to the Disasters Emergency Committee (DEC) appeal after the Boxing Day earthquake and tsunami in the Indian Ocean. The British public raised £25m in two days; at one point, donations were being received at a rate of £15,000 a minute.

30th December, 2004

This £1.42m, 150-tonne steel sculpture, designed by Thomas Heatherwick and called the 'B of the Bang', was created to commemorate the 2002 Commonwealth Games and erected outside the City of Manchester Stadium. Unfortunately, the 184ft (56m) tall structure began to fall apart and had to be fenced off for safety. Eventually, Manchester City Council sued Heatherwick and his contractors, being awarded £1.7m in damages.
12th January, 2005

Ellen MacArthur celebrates on board her yacht *B&Q/Castorama*. She had just smashed the record for the fastest person to sail single-handedly around the world non-stop, having completed the journey in 71 days, 14 hours, 18 minutes and 33 seconds. For her achievement, she was made a Dame Commander of the Order of the British Empire (DBE); she is thought to be the youngest recipient of the honour. She was also made a Chevalier of the Légion d'Honneur by French President Sarkozy.

8th February, 2005

The image of a medal displaying the slogan "*London 2012 Candidate City*" is projected on to Big Ben. Similar images also would appear on other famous London landmarks, such as Tower Bridge and the Shell Building, as the London 2012 bidding team entertained the International Olympic Committee (IOC) in their attempt to win the Olympic Games for London.

18th February, 2005

Pensive mood. England
football manager
Sven Göran Eriksson
contemplates the coming
World Cup Qualifier with
Azerbaijan at St James'
Park, Newcastle upon Tyne.
England would win the
match 2–0.
29th March, 2005

A priest in the Pro-Cathedral, at a Solemn Mass of Remembrance for the late Pope John Paul II, who had died on 2nd April, 2005, at the age of 85.
5th April, 2005

Thousands of people gather
in Trafalgar Square before
setting off on a candle-lit
procession to Westminster
Cathedral in memory of
Pope John Paul II.
7th April, 2005

Facing page: The Prince of
Wales and the Duchess of
Cornwall, formerly Camilla
Parker-Bowles, greet
well-wishers after their civil
wedding ceremony at the
Guildhall, Windsor.
9th April, 2005

Action man. Conservative leader Michael Howard prepares to address his party in the run-up to the General Election. The Conservatives failed to oust the Labour government, although did shrink its majority. Howard would resign as leader of the party in December 2005, saying that he would be too old to lead it into another General Election.
13th April, 2005

British Prime Minister Tony Blair and his wife, Cherie, arrive back at 10 Downing Street, after the Labour Party had won a historic third term in office, albeit with a reduced majority. Blair would remain in office for another two years before handing over the premiership to Chancellor Gordon Brown.
6th May, 2005

Chelsea manager
Jose Mourinho lifts the
Premiership trophy in
celebration with Frank
Lampard (L), John Terry (R)
and the rest of the team.
They had beaten Liverpool to
the cup after extra time.
7th May, 2005

Actors (L–R) James Lomas, George McGuire and Liam Mower during a curtain call for the world premiere of *Billy Elliot, The Musical*. The show was based on the 2000 film *Billy Elliot* and featured music by Sir Elton John.
12th May, 2005

Queen Elizabeth II sits next to Chief Alphonse Bird of the
Federation of Indian Nations, at the First Nations University
in Regina, Saskatchewan. The city, which was celebrating its
centennial, welcomed the Queen on the first day of her nine-
day state visit to Canada.
17th May, 2005

Iron man. A dog seems puzzled by one of a hundred life-size, cast-iron, naked figures that form 'Another Place', the latest work of art by Antony Gormley, renowned for his 'Angel of the North'. The figures are dotted across Crosby beach near Liverpool.

14th June, 2005

Pride of place. Revellers taking part in the annual Pride
Parade through London. The organizers of the event were
expecting the huge numbers of people attending the Live 8
concert in Hyde Park to swell the parade.
2nd July, 2005

Co-organizer Sir Bob Geldof on stage at Live 8. The benefit
concert was one of several held around the world just before
the G8 Conference in Scotland, with the aim of supporting
the Make Poverty History campaign.
2nd July, 2005

Robbie Williams performs on stage during the Live 8 concert in Hyde Park, London. Williams began his set with the Queen classic, *We Will Rock You* as a tribute to Freddie Mercury.
2nd July, 2005

Police clash with protesters in Princess Street, Edinburgh, as anti-capitalism demonstrators take to the streets of Scotland's capital ahead of the forthcoming meeting of G8 leaders in Gleneagles.

4th July, 2005

Splattered in blood, an injured man leaves Edgware Road Underground station, having been caught up in a terrorist bomb outrage. Four British Muslims, incensed by the country's involvement in the Iraq War, had carried out a co-ordinated series of suicide attacks on the public transport system during the morning rush hour. At 8.50am, three bombs exploded within 50 seconds of each other on separate Underground trains; a fourth exploded an hour later on a double-decker bus in Tavistock Square. In addition to themselves, the '7/7' bombers killed 52 and injured around 700.

7th July, 2005

The remains of the double-decker bus in Tavistock Square, London, following the terrorist bomb explosion of 7th July. The bomb had exploded toward the rear of the upper deck, leaving the front largely intact. Most of the passengers at the front of the bus survived, as did the driver. The remainder took the brunt of the explosion. The bomber was identified as Hasib Hussain from Leeds. The Underground train bombers were Mohammad Sidique Khan from Dewsbury, Shehzad Tanweer from Leeds and Germaine Lindsay from Aylesbury.
8th July, 2005

Facing page: Poppies flutter down over Buckingham Palace and the crowds packing the Mall at the end of a day of events commemorating the 60th anniversary of the end of the Second World War. A million poppies had been dropped during a flypast by the country's only surviving airworthy Lancaster bomber.
10th July, 2005

A candle is lit in memory of Jean Charles de Menezes during a vigil outside London's Stockwell Underground station. The vigil was held by friends and supporters of the Brazilian electrician, who had been shot dead at the station by police, having been mistaken for a suicide bomber in the aftermath of a series of failed public transport bombings on 21st July, 2005.
25th July, 2005

Party spirit. A reveller dances with a reluctant policeman during the Notting Hill Carnival in west London. The streets were packed as thousands danced in blazing sunshine on the final and busiest day of the carnival.
29th August, 2005

Under a shower of confetti, the England cricket team celebrates during the Ashes victory parade in Trafalgar Square, London. England had regained the Ashes on the previous day after drawing the final Test match and winning the series 2–1. That year's series of matches had been closely fought, many fans considering them to be the most exciting cricket in living memory.

13th September, 2005

England cricketers (L–R) Andrew Flintoff (with daughter
Holly), Kevin Pietersen and Michael Vaughan celebrate
winning the Ashes on the team bus during the victory parade
through London.
13th September, 2005

A pensive Charles Kennedy, leader of the Liberal Democrats, prepares the speech he will give to the party during its annual conference in Blackpool. In late 2005, Kennedy would come under increasing criticism for his leadership style. This, compounded by an admission of a drink problem, would see him lose the support of the parliamentary party, and he would resign on 7th January, 2006.

21st September, 2005

Grasping a thorny issue.
Britain's Chancellor, Gordon
Brown, makes a point during
the Labour Party conference
in Brighton.
26th September, 2005

Facing page: Visitors
inspect Turner Prize-winning
artist Rachel Whiteread's
new installation, titled
'Embankment', inside the
Tate Modern's Turbine Hall in
London. The work comprises
14,000 translucent white
polyethylene boxes, cast
from the inside of cardboard
boxes and stacked in a
variety of manners.
10th October, 2005

Looking for all the world like a war zone, the car park
at Northgate on the Maylands Industrial Park, Hemel
Hempstead, Hertfordshire is a scene of complete devastation
following an explosion and fire at the nearby Buncefield
oil storage depot. Hundreds of homes in the area were
evacuated and around 2,000 people had to find alternative
accommodation until the emergency services brought the
blaze under control.
14th December, 2005

Chris Martin of Coldplay performs on stage at the Earls Court Exhibition Centre, west London during the band's UK tour.
14th December, 2005

Shannon Sickles (L) and Grainne Close arrive at Belfast City Hall as the first civil partnership ceremonies for gay couples in the UK are held in Northern Ireland. Almost 700 gay 'marriages' would take place across England and Wales over the following few days, when arrangements for the new civil partnerships came fully into operation. The registration period was shorter in Northern Ireland, allowing same-sex couples in the province to form civil partnerships earlier than those on the mainland.

19th December, 2005

Sir Elton John and his partner, David Furnish, wave to well-wishers outside Windsor Guildhall after their civil partnership ceremony.
21st December, 2005

Double delight for steam enthusiasts. The *Christmas Dalesman* train took to the famous Settle to Carlisle railway line and crossed the dramatic Ribblehead Viaduct hauled by two steam engines, the LMS Stanier Class 5 4-6-0 locomotive No. 45407, *Lancashire Fusilier* and British Railways Standard 4 2-6-0 locomotive No. 76079 (in front).
21st December, 2005

Tradition lives on. Despite the apparent ban on hunting with dogs imposed by the 2004 Hunting Act, traditional Boxing Day gatherings of local hunts and their packs take place all over the country. The ambiguities contained within the Act mean that little has actually changed for those who want to ride to hounds.

26th December, 2005

American model Paris Hilton and Welsh fashion designer Julien Macdonald celebrate the climax of Macdonald's show for London Fashion Week (autumn/winter season), at the Freemason's Hall, central London.
14th February, 2006

Golden girls. Rapper Kanye West makes a glittering entrance
at the Brit Awards, Earls Court, west London. West would
pick up the award for Best International Male Solo Artist.
15th February, 2006

Darling daughters. Bob Geldof's daughters, (L–R) Tiger Lilly, Pixie and Peaches, are overjoyed as their father receives the Freedom of Dublin City in a special ceremony outside the Mansion House in Dublin.
5th March, 2006

They say that owners often begin to look like their dogs. A doberman and owner await their turn in the ring during the Crufts annual dog show at the National Exhibition Centre, Birmingham. Over 24,000 dogs from 32 countries would gather for the event, which is in its 115th year. Tens of thousands of visitors would attend over the four days of competition.
8th March, 2006

Trooper Saulailai of the Royal Scots Dragoon Guards holds an SA80 rifle as he looks through the window of a Land Rover while on patrol on the banks of the Shaat Al Arab River in Basra, southern Iraq.
28th March, 2006

Happy birthday, Ma'am. Queen Elizabeth II sits in the Regency Room at Buckingham Palace, reading some of the cards that have been sent to her on her 80th birthday.
20th April, 2006

A forest of sails marks the progress of competitors in the
75th Round The Island Race, as they negotiate The Needles
lighthouse on the western tip of the Isle of Wight. Over 1,600
yachts of all sizes would take part in the annual race.
3rd June, 2006

Zara Phillips, daughter of Princess Anne and Mark Phillips, tackles the water jump on Ardfield Magic Star at the Bramham International Horse Trials, Bramham Park, West Yorkshire.
10th June, 2006

Red card. England's Wayne Rooney (R) is sent off for a foul on Portugal's Alberto Ricardo Carvalho by referee Horacio Marcelo Elizondo during the World Cup quarter-final. The match would end 0–0, but England would lose a penalty shootout 3–1.

1st July, 2006

The RAF's Red Arrows display team demonstrate their skills in formation flying during the International Air Tattoo at Fairford in Gloucestershire.
15th July, 2006

Tears of joy. US golfer Tiger Woods sheds tears after winning the 135th Open Championship at the Royal Liverpool Golf Club, Hoylake. One of the most successful professional golfers of all time, Woods has won 14 major championships and 71 PGA tour events. At the end of 2009, revelations of infidelity would cause him to take a break from the sport for several months to focus on his marriage.
23rd July, 2006

A rainbow peace flag flutters in the wind as protesters gather outside the gates of the USAF base at RAF Mildenhall, in Suffolk, to demonstrate against flights carrying weapons from the United States to Israel, where they were thought to be used in attacks against civilian targets in Lebanon.
31st July, 2006

Facing page: Don't look now. A security guard keeps watch on the latest work by hyper-realist sculptor Ron Mueck, which is on display at the Royal Scottish Academy building, Edinburgh. The 9ft (2.7m) tall representation of a naked human, titled 'Wild Man', is just one of many realistic sculptures created by the Australian-born artist.
4th August, 2006

The moors are ablaze with purple heather as riders in the Tour of Britain cycle race climb through the Trough of Bowland, near Preston. The annual event comprises a number of stages in which riders race from place to place across the country.
30th August, 2006

Facing page: A woman contemplates Bridget Riley's 1961 work, 'Movement in Squares', at an exhibition called 'How to Improve the World: 60 Years of British Art', at the Hayward Gallery in the South Bank Centre, central London.
5th September, 2006

Demonstrators clutching black balloons play dead during an anti-war protest march in Manchester.
23rd September, 2006

Babyshambles lead singer Pete Doherty and his girlfriend, model Kate Moss, arrive at Dublin Airport for the band's gig in Carlow. Doherty had a tumultuous on-off relationship with Moss, not helped by problems of drug abuse.
25th September, 2006

Pop group Girls Aloud at the BBC Radio 1 Chart Show Live, held at the Brighton Dome, Brighton, Sussex. L–R: Nadine Coyle, Cheryl Cole, Sarah Harding, Nicola Roberts and Kimberley Walsh. The group had been created by the television talent show *Popstars: The Rivals* in 2002.

12th November, 2006

Members of PETA (People for the Ethical Treatment
of Animals) invade Burberry's shop on Regent Street
in London in protest at the company's use of real
fur. Demonstrators managed to gain access to the
shop's windows, smearing them with fake blood and
displaying posters.
16th November, 2006

Facing page: WPC Teresa Milburn (C, face
concealed) is consoled by two colleagues during
a memorial service for fellow officer Sharon
Beshenivsky in Bradford. Beshenivsky and Milburn
had been called to a robbery in Bradford on 18th
November, 2005, and both had been shot by the
Somali gang carrying out the raid, the former fatally.
Five of the robbers have since been put behind bars.
18th November, 2006

Members of the pop group Take That, (L–R) Gary Barlow, Howard Donald, Mark Owen and Jason Orange, at RAF Northolt, on the stairs of a private jet ferrying them between CD signing sessions in London and Manchester. Originally, the boy band had included Robbie Williams, but he left in 1995 and the group disbanded in the following year. They reformed in 2005.
27th November, 2006

Noel Gallagher performs in the home of Oasis fan Ben Hayes in Stockport. Hayes had won a competition on BBC Radio 1 and said of the private concert, *"He was just sat in my lounge, playing three songs. It was just the best day of my life – so far."*

1st December, 2006

Eyes front. Queen Elizabeth II inspects Army officer graduates during the Sovereign's Parade at Sandhurst Royal Military Academy at Camberley in Surrey. Trying hard not to giggle is her grandson, Prince William.

15th December, 2006

A young member of a herd of Highland cattle gets a taste of the cold stuff after heavy snowfall at Carronbridge, near Denny in Scotland.
18th January, 2007

The stricken cargo ship MSC *Napoli*, aground just off Branscombe Beach, near Sidmouth, Devon. As the containers began to be washed from the ship and on to the beach, a salvage free-for-all took place, with people turning up from as far away as the Midlands, intent on plundering the scattered cargo. All manner of goods were washed up, including motorcycles, wine casks, dog food and cosmetics.

23rd January, 2007

Conflicts in Iraq and Afghanistan, together with suicide
bombings in London, caused tensions with Britain's Muslim
communities, and extremists on both sides sought to stoke
up animosity. These three women in Spark Hill, Birmingham
show their contempt of the camera.
31st January, 2007

The **2000s** Britain in Pictures

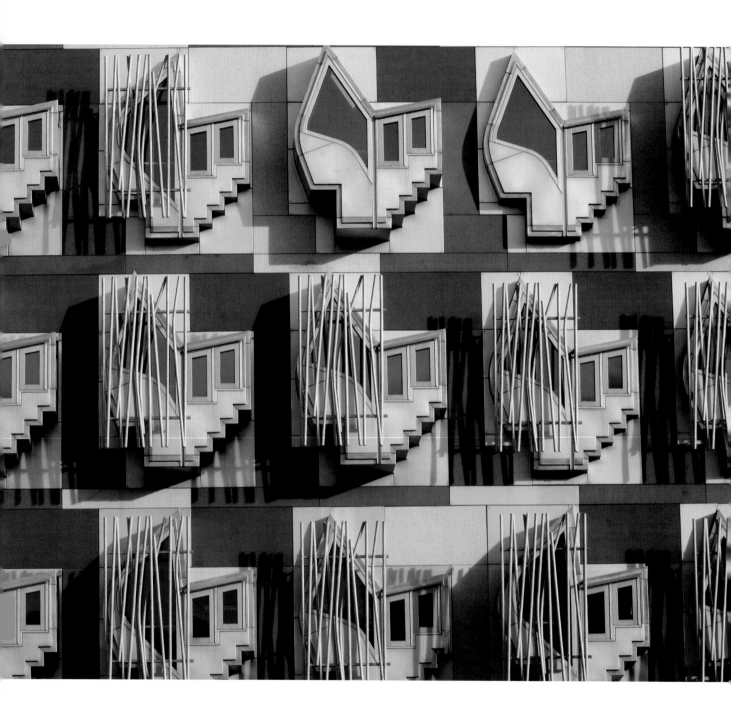

Facing page: The striking architectural detail of the Scottish Parliament building at Holyrood, Edinburgh. Designed by Catalan architect Enric Miralles, who died before its completion, the building was opened by Queen Elizabeth II on 9th October, 2004. Although controversial and not well-received by all, the building has won a number of awards, including the 2005 Stirling Prize.
31st January, 2007

Respect. Leader of the Conservative Party David Cameron (L) walks through the Benchill area of Wythenshawe during a visit to Manchester. Behind him, Ryan Florence, 17, shows his feelings about the politician by making a gun gesture.
22nd February, 2007

How long to rain over us?
Queen Elizabeth II shelters
from a shower during the
official opening of the
Lawn Tennis Association's
new state-of-the-art
National Tennis Centre at
Roehampton, south-west
London. The facility has 22
indoor and outdoor courts, a
gymnasium, outdoor sprint
track, and hydrotherapy and
plunge pools.
29th March, 2007

Irish U2 singer Bono shows appreciation for his honorary knighthood at the British Ambassador's official residence in Sandyford, Dublin. He was given the award for his humanitarian efforts.
29th March, 2007

Tattooed lady. Singer-songwriter Amy Winehouse performs during an exclusive Vodafone TBA concert at Circomedia in Bristol. Known for her powerful contralto vocals, Winehouse was the first British singer to win five Grammys, including Best New Artist, Record of the Year and Song of the Year (all for her second album, *Back to Black*, in 2006). Her problems with drugs and her self-destructive behaviour, however, have gained her much media attention.

19th April, 2007

Salvation for the lost. For those unable to find their way with the aid of a map, the satellite navigation (SatNav) system is a boon. Stick it on the windscreen, plug it in and a soothing voice tells you where to go. Early examples did have flaws in their databases, however, leading unsuspecting motorists into forays along one-way streets in the wrong direction and truck drivers to attempt to negotiate lanes that were far too narrow for their charges.

25th April, 2007

People gather for Umbrella Action Day on Sandymount Strand, Dublin. Promoted by the Stop Climate Chaos Coalition, the event was intended to send a message to the Irish government that firm action was required to tackle climate change.
10th May, 2007

Kate McCann looks at a large *News of the World* poster of her missing daughter, Madeleine, on the beach in Praia da Luz, Portugal, where the child went missing shortly before her fourth birthday. No trace of her has ever been found.
28th May, 2007

Cider with Lily. Can in hand, Lily Allen performs on the Pyramid Stage during the 2007 Glastonbury Festival, at Worthy Farm in Pilton, Somerset. It was not her first visit: at the age of 14, she had run away from home to attend the festival.

23rd June, 2007

Having inherited the post from Tony Blair, who had resigned, new Prime Minister Gordon Brown and his wife, Sarah, take possession of their official residence, 10 Downing Street.
27th June, 2007

Last gasp. Punters in a south London pub savour their last cigarettes and cigars, and take a final puff of their pipe, before the smoking ban in all public places throughout Britain comes into force on 1st July, 2007.
30th June, 2007

Sir Elton John performs during a charity concert at Wembley Stadium, London in memory of
Diana, Princess of Wales on what would have been her 46th birthday.
1st July, 2007

Police forensic investigators at the scene of the terrorist attack at Glasgow Airport, where a car laden with gas cylinders had been driven into the terminal building and set on fire by two Muslim extremists. Prompt action by the emergency services, police and members of the public prevented an explosion and saw both men apprehended, one, Kafeel Ahmed, with severe burns from which he would die some weeks later. The other terrorist was Bilal Abdullah, a doctor, who received a 32-year sentence for attempted murder.
1st July, 2007

Riders pass the Clock Tower of the Palace of Westminster as they leave London on the first stage of the Tour de France, London to Canterbury. This was the third occasion on which the famous cycle race had visited England.
8th July, 2007

Facing page: Members of 9 Regiment, Army Air Corps (AAC) receive campaign medals for service in Afghanistan from the Prince of Wales, colonel-in-chief of the regiment, during a ceremony at Clarence House, London. The AAC provides helicopter support for ground troops.

11th July, 2007

Supporters of Dr Andrew Wakefield, and Professors John Walker-Smith and Simon Murch outside a General Medical Council hearing in central London. In 1998, the three men had published a report suggesting that the combined measles, mumps and rubella (MMR) vaccination was responsible for children developing autism. Their study caused one of the biggest health scares in years, led to a drop in the take-up of the MMR vaccination and resulted in a rise in cases of measles. Ultimately, the study would be discredited.

16th July, 2007

J.K. Rowling at the launch of *Harry Potter and the Deathly Hallows* at The Natural History Museum in London. The novel was the seventh and last in the Harry Potter series. Released in 93 countries simultaneously, it became the fastest selling book of all time, 15,000,000 copies being sold within the first 24 hours.
20th July, 2007

Tewkesbury Abbey and a substantial part of the Gloucestershire town are marooned on an island following torrential rain during the previous 24 hours. The town stands at the confluence of the River Severn and River Avon, and inundation of the surrounding flood plain is common; only rarely does it affect the town itself.
22nd July, 2007

Members of a Welsh Guards
mortar platoon open fire on
Taliban positions in support
of an operation carried
out by the Worcestershire
and Sherwood Foresters
Regiment in Helmand
Province, Afghanistan.
16th August, 2007

Great Britain's Christine Ohuruogu proudly shows her gold medal after winning the 400m event during the IAAF World Championships in Osaka, Japan. She would go on to win a gold medal in the event at the 2008 Beijing Olympics.
29th August, 2007

Keira Knightley at the premiere of *Atonement* during the 64th Venice International Film Festival. Knightly had starred in the film alongside James McAvoy. *Atonement* received the award for Best Film of the Year at the 61st British Academy Film awards.
29th August, 2007

In sombre mood, Princes Charles, William and Harry leave
a Service of Thanksgiving for the life of Diana, Princess of
Wales at the Guards' Chapel, London.
31st August, 2007

Boris Johnson, former MP for Henley-on-Thames and ex-editor of *The Spectator*, who had been named Tory candidate for the 2008 London mayoral contest, at a media briefing at the Conservative Party Central Office, London. Johnson would go on to win the election, ousting former mayor Ken Livingstone.
27th September, 2007

In the zone. McLaren Mercedes driver Lewis Hamilton focuses his thoughts ahead of the Brazilian Grand Prix at Interlagos, São Paulo, Brazil, the last race of the Formula One season. He was four championship points ahead of his nearest rival, Kimi Räikkönen, but a gearbox problem during the race would consign him to seventh place, while Räikkönen would win, taking the championship. However, Hamilton would become world champion in 2008.
21st October, 2007

Harry Patch, 109, from Wells, Somerset is the guest of honour in Weston-super-Mare during the launch of the local poppy appeal. Patch was the last surviving soldier to have fought in the trenches of the First World War and had recently published his autobiography, *The Last Fighting Tommy*. He would die in July 2009, at the age of 111.
27th October, 2007

A building in Bethnal Green,
east London displays
artwork allegedly painted by
graffiti artist Banksy.
31st October, 2007

Facing page: Trains at
the new Eurostar terminal,
recently opened by Queen
Elizabeth II at St Pancras
Station in London.
The terminal had been
completed as part of an
£800m refurbishment of
the famous building.
6th November, 2007

Playwright Harold Pinter
arrives for the UK premiere
of the film *Sleuth* at the
Odeon West End in
Leicester Square, central
London. The film, which
starred Michael Caine and
Jude Law, was based on
his screenplay of Anthony
Shaffer's award winning play
of the same name. Pinter
would die from liver cancer
at the end of 2008.
18th November, 2007

The arch that supports the roof of the new Wembley Stadium makes a dramatic statement against the night sky. The stadium had been handed over to the Football Association in March 2007, in time for that year's FA Cup Final. It has a 90,000 capacity and is the second largest stadium in Europe.

21st November, 2007

Facing page: Clash and splash. Derby County's Tyrone Mears (L) and Manchester United's Wayne Rooney battle for the ball as the rain pours down. United would win 4–1.

8th December, 2007

Yellow labrador Endal, an assistance dog who was awarded one of the first PDSA (People's Dispensary for Sick Animals) Gold Medals, in 2002, for bravery and devotion to duty during a ceremony at the newly restored Ilford Animal Cemetery, in east London. Endal had pulled his disabled owner into the recovery position after he had been struck by a car, covered him with a blanket and pushed his mobile phone against his face. When his owner recovered consciousness, the dog left him to seek help.
13th December, 2007

Facing page: The skyscrapers of Canary Wharf in London's Docklands development emerge above a sea of fog that has engulfed the surrounding landscape.
11th February, 2008

Kleber Afonso sits in his study in Wombwell, Barnsley, South Yorkshire, where part of the roof had collapsed during the previous night's earthquake. The tremor hit at around 1am and was measured at a magnitutde of 5.2.
27th February, 2008

Prince Harry, having been commissioned a second
lieutenant in the Blues and Royals of the Household Cavalry
Regiment, mans a 50mm machine gun during a spell of
active service in Helmand Province, southern Afghanistan.
28th February, 2008

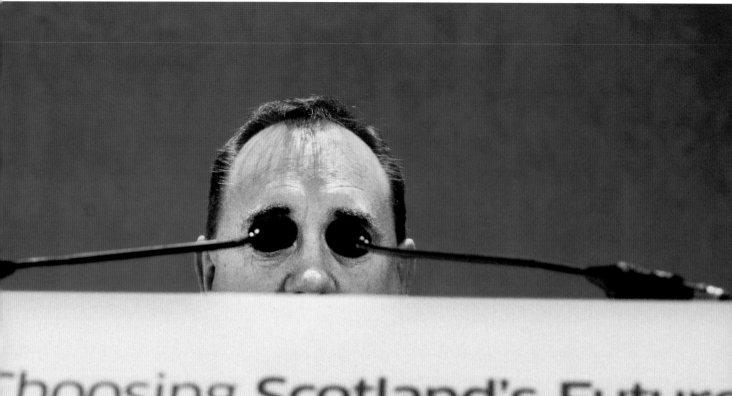

Eyes on the future. Scotland's First Minister, Alex Salmond,
leader of the Scottish National Party, at Edinburgh University
during his National Conversation on the constitution.
26th March, 2008

Welsh boxer Joe Calzaghe during an open workout at the Newbridge Gym, Abercarn. Calzaghe would retire from the ring in February 2009 an undefeated champion, having won all 46 of his professional fights.
26th March, 2008

Actor David Tennant arrives for the screening of the fourth series of the BBC's hit television show *Doctor Who*, at the Apollo West End in central London. Tennant played the tenth incarnation of the famous time lord from 2005 to 2010.

1st April, 2008

Britain's Prime Minister Gordon Brown waits to address the
United Nations Security Council at the UN headquarters in
New York, during discussions on Resolution 1809, Peace
and Security in Africa.
16th April, 2008

Writers James Corden and Ruth Jones with the Programme of The Year award for their sitcom, *Gavin and Stacey*, at the British Academy Television Awards at the London Palladium. In addition to writing the series, the pair took major roles in it.
20th April, 2008

Over the moon. Manchester United's manager, Alex Ferguson, celebrates at the final whistle after his team had beaten Spanish side Barcelona 1–0.
29th April, 2008

Beaten man. Former London Mayor Ken Livingstone leaves City Hall in London with a carrier bag after meeting his successor, Conservative Boris Johnson. Labour politician Livingstone had held the post for eight years. He had also acted as leader of the Greater London Council between 1981 and 1986, when it was abolished by Margaret Thatcher's government, and had served as MP for Brent East.
9th May, 2008

The continuation of a warm spell of weather packed Brighton
Beach in East Sussex with sunbathers.
11th May, 2008

The RAF Battle of Britain Memorial Flight's Lancaster
bomber, one of only two airworthy examples in the world,
flies over the Derwent Dam, in the Peak District, to mark the
65th anniversary of the Second World War 'Dambusters'
raid. The dam was used by 617 Squadron, led by Guy
Gibson, to practise its attack on the German Ruhr dams with
'bouncing' bombs.
16th May, 2008

Chris Hoy, a member of Great Britain's Olympic cycling team. The multiple world champion would win three gold medals at the 2008 Olympics in Beijing, the first Briton to do so in a hundred years. Having already been awarded an MBE for his services to cycling (in 2005), he was knighted for his achievements by Queen Elizabeth II in 2009.

24th July, 2008

Tom Daley during a practice dive at the National Aquatics Centre, Beijing. At 14, he was Great Britain's youngest competitor at the 2008 Olympics, specializing in the 10m platform event. In the individual competition, he was seventh, while in the synchronized event, he placed eighth with partner Blake Aldridge.
7th August, 2008

Facing page: Was that the one about the man with incredibly hairy knees? The Prince of Wales and his consort, the Duchess of Cornwall, enjoy the Mey Highland Games in Caithness, Scotland.
9th August, 2008

Flying the flag. Christine Ohuruogu is overjoyed after winning gold in the Women's 400m at the National Stadium at the 2008 Beijing Olympic Games in China.
19th August, 2008

Facing page: Great Britain's Rebecca Romero celebrates winning the gold medal in the Women's Individual Pursuit cycling event at the Laoshan Velodrome during the 2008 Beijing Olympic Games in China. Romero has won world championships in both rowing and cycling.
17th August, 2008

Facing page: Prime Minister Gordon Brown takes part in a question-and-answer session during the first day of the 2008 Labour Party Conference in Manchester.
20th September, 2008

With a deafening roar, and trailing red, white and blue smoke, the RAF's crack aerobatic team, the Red Arrows, flies over the Tyne Bridge to give a rousing send-off to the competitors in the BUPA Great North Run in Newcastle. The event is the most popular half-marathon road race in the world, participants running from Newcastle upon Tyne to South Shields.
5th October, 2008

An office worker watches the FTSE 100 on the day that bank shares plunge, following the revelation that many major financial institutions may need government assistance. After a meeting between the bosses of the major UK banks and Chancellor Alistair Darling on the previous day, the chancellor, Prime Minister Gordon Brown and Bank of England Governor Mervyn King meet to determine a plan of action to stabilize the financial system.
7th October, 2008

In the wake of the financial crisis, many businesses go under, including familiar household and high-street names. Closing-down sales become commonplace and unemployment rises.
8th October, 2008

Beneath a shower of confetti and to public acclaim, Great
Britain's Olympic athletes are welcomed home from Beijing
with a celebration in Trafalgar Square, London.
16th October, 2008

The judges from the ITV talent show *The X Factor*, (L–R) Simon Cowell, Cheryl Cole and Louis Walsh, at the 2008 National Television Awards at London's Royal Albert Hall. The show would lose out to the BBC's *Strictly Come Dancing* in the Most Popular Talent Show category. Cowell, however, would receive a Special Recognition Award.
29th October, 2008

Tributes are left for Peter Connelly, the abused 17-month-old infant known initially only as Baby P, at the site where his ashes were scattered at Islington Crematorium in north London. The little boy had died as a result of more than 50 injuries received during an eight-month period from his mother, her boyfriend and her boyfriend's brother, despite having been seen repeatedly by social workers.
19th November, 2008

Protesters demonstrate outside the Israeli Embassy in Kensington, London, against Israel's continuing military action in the Gaza Strip, which forms part of the Palestinian territories. On 27th December, Israeli F-16 strike fighters had attacked police stations, schools, hospitals, UN warehouses and government buildings in the Gaza Strip, apparently in retaliation for Palestinian rocket attacks on southern Israel.

31st December, 2008

Timber galore. The beach at Ramsgate in Kent is covered
with thousands of wooden planks, after they had been
washed from the decks of a Russian freighter, the *Sinegorsk*,
which got into trouble during a storm in the English Channel.
22nd January, 2009

Stars of the television sitcom *Gavin and Stacey*, (L–R) Ruth Jones, Rob Brydon and Joanna Page, at the launch of Comic Relief's 2009 Red Nose Day charity appeal, outside the Empire Leicester Square, London. By 2nd July, £80m would have been raised from institutions and the public.
29th January, 2009

Heavy snowfall hits the UK, but it's still walkies as usual for this dog and its owner in Chiswick, west London. Some areas of London had up to 8in (200mm) of snow; all London bus services were suspended, while there were severe delays on the Underground system.
2nd February, 2009

Florence Welch of Florence and the Machine performs on stage during the NME Shockwaves Award Tour at Rock City in Nottingham.
11th February, 2009

Jade Goody and Jack Tweed kiss on the driveway of her home in Upshire, Essex on the eve of their wedding. The celebrity had terminal cancer and would die a month later, on 22nd March.

21st February, 2009

Pop star Michael Jackson announces plans for his upcoming concert in London in July, at the O2 Arena on the Greenwich peninsula. The singer would die from a drugs overdose, however, at his Los Angeles home on 25th June.
5th March, 2009

Home Secretary Jacqui Smith leaves her south London home after it had been revealed by the *Sunday Express* that she had claimed expenses from the Commons for the rental of two adult films from Virgin Media. Subsequently, it was announced that she had broken the rules on second-home expenses and was ordered to apologize. She stood down from her government post after a Cabinet reshuffle in June.
30th March, 2009

Prime Minister Gordon Brown and recently elected US President Barack Obama shake hands during a press conference at the Foreign and Commonwealth Office in London. Obama was in London to attend the G20 Summit meeting called to address the global financial crisis.

1st April, 2009

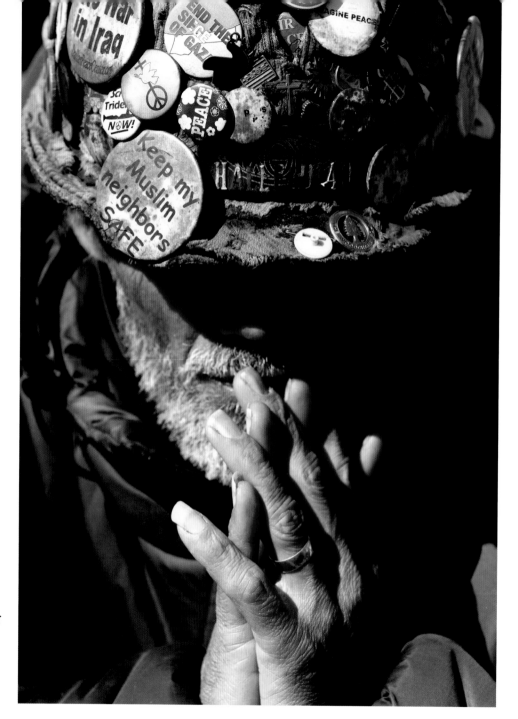

Anti-war protester Brian Haw joins demonstrators campaigning against the Sri Lankan government's offensive against Tamil Tiger rebels and alleged human rights abuses, outside the Houses of Parliament in central London.

8th April, 2009

The eternal flame at the Hillsborough Memorial in Liverpool's Town Hall. Ninety-six Liverpool fans had died at the home of Sheffield Wednesday during an FA Cup semi-final on 15th April, 1989. A surge of fans trying to get into the stadium had caused those at the front of the crowd to be crushed against the barriers that prevented an invasion of the pitch. The disaster led to many stadiums being converted to all-seat venues.
14th April, 2009

Economic migrants at a camp in the French port of Calais receive food handouts from a local charity. The men, from many different countries, were hoping to find a way across the English Channel to the UK. Many would attempt to smuggle themselves in by hiding in the backs of lorries.
17th April, 2009

Work proceeds on the 2012
Olympic Stadium in east
London. With a planned
capacity of 80,000, the stadium
will host the track and field
athletics as well as the opening
and closing ceremonies.
21st April, 2009

Best foot forward. Prime Minister Gordon Brown arrives at Lashkar Gah, a forward base in Helmand Province, Afghanistan, where he is due to take part in a meeting with locals and community leaders. The conflict in the country would be a continuing concern for his premiership.
27th April, 2009

Campaigner Joanna Lumley, whose father had served as an officer with the 6th Gurkha Rifles, celebrates outside the House of Commons in Westminster, where it had been announced that Gurkha soldiers from Nepal would gain full UK residency rights.
21st May, 2009

The band Elbow at the 54th Ivor Novello Awards, Grosvenor House, Park Lane, London, where two of their songs received awards: *One Day Like This* for Best Song Musically and Lyrically; and *Grounds for Divorce* for Best Contemporary Song.
21st May, 2009

Facing page: Yayoi Kusama's signature work, 'Ascension of Polkadots', part of the Hayward Gallery's 2009 summer exhibition 'Walking in My Mind', at the South Bank, London.
22nd June, 2009

Great Britain's Andy Murray in action against Switzerland's
Stanislas Wawrinka in the fourth round of the Men's Singles
at Wimbledon. Their match was the first full game to be
played with the centre court's new retractable roof closed.
29th June, 2009

Andy Murray celebrates his victory over Stanislas Wawrinka during the Wimbledon Championships. Their match had continued after dark thanks to the floodlights mounted in the centre court's roof. Murray would make it through to the semi-finals, where he would lose to Andy Roddick.
29th June, 2009

L–R: Rupert Grint (Ron Weasley), Emma Watson (Hermione Granger) and Daniel Radcliffe (Harry Potter) arrive for the world premiere of the film *Harry Potter and the Half-Blood Prince*, at the Odeon Leicester Square, London. The film was the sixth installment in the Harry Potter series.

7th July, 2009

Work continues on a gigantic bonfire built from pallets in Newtownabbey, outside Belfast. Similar fires will be set alight across Northern Ireland on 11th July, or Eleventh Night, on the eve of The Twelfth, also known as Orangemen's Day. The Protestant celebration commemorates the victory of King William of Orange over the Catholic King James II at the Battle of the Boyne.
10th July, 2009

Clad in one of her trademark eye-catching costumes, American singer Lady Gaga performs at the T in the Park music festival in Balado, Perth and Kinross, Scotland. The annual festival, held since 1994, spans three days in July. In 2009, there were over 180 acts and a crowd of 85,000.

11th July, 2009

England bowler Andrew 'Freddie' Flintoff celebrates with his team mates after his five-wicket haul against Australia during the second Test of the 2009 Ashes series. Former captain Flintoff had announced that he would be retiring from Test cricket after the series, which England won 2–1.
20th July, 2009

Facing page: Thames Water engineer Rob Smith examines part of London's sewer network during the company's 'Bin it – don't block it' campaign to stop sewer abuse. Sewer blockages often occur because people flush inappropriate items down the toilet or sink drains, leading to unpleasant flooding.
5th August, 2009

At Wembley Stadium, a minute's applause is held before the kick-off between Manchester United and Chelsea, in memory of Sir Bobby Robson, who had died on 31st July, at the age of 76. Robson had enjoyed a 20-year career as a player with Fulham, West Bromwich Albion and Vancouver, and had played for England on 20 occasions. Subsequently, he went on to become a successful club and international manager.
9th August, 2009

Sir Bobby Robson
1933 – 2009

20,000 coaches trained by 2010

Out! England's Jonathan Trott is run out by Australia's Simon Katich during the fifth npower Test Match at the Oval, London. England would go on to win the match, however, by 197 runs and would regain the Ashes.

20th August, 2009

England captain Andrew Strauss lifts the trophy through a shower of champagne, following victory over Australia in the fifth npower Test Match at the Oval, London.

23rd August, 2009

All steamed up. Don Wales, driver of the British Steam Car, leaps for joy after averaging 148.308mph in two runs across Rogers Dry Lake on Edwards Air Force Base in California's Mojave Desert, to break the land speed record for a steam powered car, which had been set by the team's other driver, Charles Burnett III, on the previous day at 139.843mph.
26th August, 2009

Concertgoers enjoy the music and celebrations during the
Last Night of the Proms at the Royal Albert Hall in London.
The Promenade concerts were founded in 1895 and take
place mainly at the Albert Hall, although other venues are
also used on the last night.
12th September, 2009

A Rembrandt masterpiece, which had not been seen in public for 40 years, at Christie's in London, where it would fetch £20.2m at auction in December. The amount was a record price for a work by the 17th-century Dutch painter.
18th September, 2009

Dedicated followers of fashion. L–R: Maggie Cheung, Dev Patel, Freida Pinto, Alexa Chung, Mary Kate Olsen, Daisy Lowe, Liv Tyler, Emma Watson and Gwyneth Paltrow at the Burberry Prorsum spring/summer show for London Fashion Week at Rootstein Hopkins Parade Ground in Chelsea College of Art & Design, London.
22nd September, 2009

An Arthur Guinness lookalike leads patrons of Belfast's
Botanic Inn in a celebration of the 250th anniversary of the
founding of the Guinness brewing business.
24th September, 2009

An old car is lifted towards a crusher, which will reduce it to a small cube of scrap metal. In May 2009, in an attempt to help the ailing car industry, the British government introduced a car scrappage scheme, whereby buyers would be entitled to £2,000 off the price of a new car if they allowed the dealer to scrap their old one, provided it was over 10 years old. Many criticized the scheme, however, as not being generous enough.
25th September, 2009

Mobile must-have. Apple's iPhone continues at the forefront
of mobile phone technology in its third incarnation, the 3GS.
Introduced in 2007, the legendary smartphone acts as a
camera phone with text messaging and visual voice mail, a
portable media player, and internet device with e-mail, web
browsing and Wi-Fi functions. With a multi-touch screen and
virtual keyboard, the iPhone's capabilities can be expanded
by the addition of thousands of third-party applications.
1st October, 2009

Saint or sinner? Former Prime Minister Tony Blair looks on in sombre mood during a reception at the Guildhall in London, following a service of commemoration at St Paul's Cathedral to honour UK military and civilian personnel who had served in Iraq. Blair had sent British forces into Iraq with the Americans to topple its dictator, Saddam Hussein. During his premiership, he ordered British troops into battle on five occasions, more than any other British prime minister in history.

9th October, 2009

Facing page: The coffin of Acting Sergeant Michael Lockett is carried from Cathcart Old Parish Church during his funeral in Glasgow. Lockett, 29, had died in Afghanistan when an improvised explosive device he was investigating exploded. In 2008, he had been awarded the Military Cross for an action in which he led other troops in an attempt to recover the bodies of two dead comrades and four other soldiers who had been wounded during a Taliban ambush. Lockett was the first holder of the Military Cross to die in Afghanistan.
15th October, 2009

Jenson Button and the Brawn GP crew celebrate winning the constructors' and drivers' Formula One championship titles at the Brazilian Grand Prix at Interlagos, São Paulo. The team, led by Ross Brawn, had made a remarkable comeback to dominate the season after previous owner Honda had walked away at the end 2008.
18th October, 2009

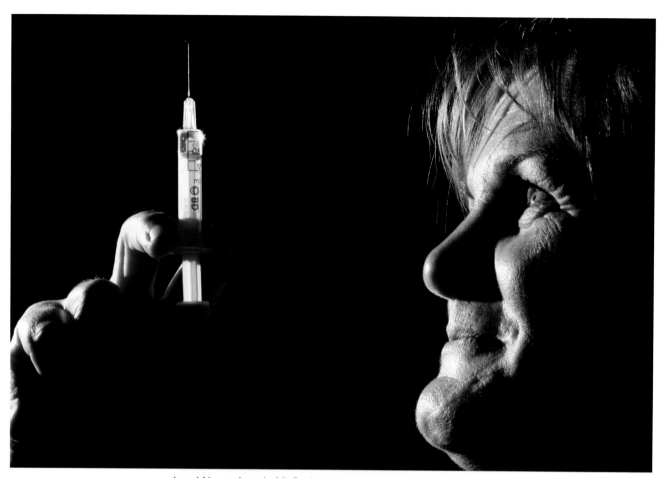

Lead Nurse Angela McGurk prepares an inoculation of
swine flu vaccine during the launch of Scotland's vaccination
programme at New Victoria Hospital in Glasgow. The fear
of a swine flue pandemic, prompted by the World Health
Organization's declaration of a *"public health emergency
of international concern"*, led to the frenzied stockpiling of
vaccines. In the event, the virus proved to be less virulent
than expected, and there were claims that it had been hyped
up by vaccine manufacturers to sell more vaccines.
21st October, 2009

A picture featuring a distorted image of British National Party (BNP) leader Nick Griffin is displayed at a Unite Against Fascism rally at Conway Hall, London, in protest against his appearance on the BBC Television *Question Time* programme on the following evening. The image had been manipulated to associate the BNP with Adolf Hitler's German Nazi Party of the 1930s and 1940s.

21st October, 2009

Following unresolved discussions between the
Communication Workers Union and the Royal Mail over
the latter's modernization plans, postal workers begin two
24-hour strikes by different segments of the workforce. The
dispute would continue until the beginning of November,
when a two-month truce would be called to protect the
Christmas mail.
22nd October, 2009

Peterborough United fans wear facemasks after an outbreak of swine flu among the Blackburn Rovers squad. The teams had met in the fourth round of the Carling Cup; despite the virus, Rovers came out on top, 5–2.

27th October, 2009

Welcome home. A hundred Riflemen of the 2nd Battalion, The Rifles march through the streets of Croydon, Surrey to the town hall to celebrate their return from a six-month operational tour in Afghanistan. Such homecoming parades had become commonplace, allowing the public to show their appreciation of the work done by the troops.
29th October, 2009

Just the ticket. Conservative leader David Cameron on his way by Underground train to the O2 Arena in London, where he would launch his 'Tickets for Troops' scheme, encouraging promoters of music concerts and sporting events to give free tickets to soldiers.
3rd November, 2009

In the light of the scandal over MP's expense claims, a giant duck house is towed past the Houses of Parliament, in a demonstration by the Vote For a Change campaign. The duck house was a large-scale copy of one claimed for by Conservative peer Sir Peter Viggers, which cost the taxpayer £1,645. The revelations about MP's expense claims led to widespread resignations among politicians, and outrage among the public.
5th November, 2009

David and Goliath. England's David Haye (R) on winning
form against Nikolai Valuev during the WBA World
Heavyweight title fight at the Nuremberg Arena, Germany.
Haye would defeat the 7ft (2.1m) Russian on points.
7th November, 2009

A gleeful David Haye celebrates becoming the new WBA World Heavyweight champion by lifting the belt after his points victory against Nikolai Valuev at the Nuremberg Arena, Germany.

7th November, 2009

A demonstrator burns a mask of former British Prime Minister Tony Blair outside the Queen Elizabeth II Conference Centre, Westminster, London, where the Iraq Inquiry would seek fresh answers concerning Blair's role in the build-up to the invasion by taking evidence from his former foreign policy adviser, Sir David Manning.

30th November, 2009

The Young Ones? Sir Cliff Richard (L) and the Shadows
(L–R) Hank Marvin, Bruce Welch and Brian Bennett, at
HMV's Oxford Street store, where they would sign copies of
their new DVD of greatest hits, *The Final Reunion*.
30th November, 2009

Protesters march along the Royal Mile, Edinburgh to the Scottish Parliament during an anti-swine flu vaccination protest. Although mandatory vaccinations had not been proposed by government, some members of the public believed a conspiracy theory involving financiers and the drug companies that such would be the case, the ultimate object being to depopulate the world.

12th December, 2009

Rocky situation. Customers queue outside a branch of the Northern Rock building society in York, as savers across the country seek to withdraw their money from the crisis-hit bank. Ultimately, the government would step in and take over the institution.

14th December, 2009

Passengers alight from a Javelin train at St Pancras Station in London on the first day of the new high-speed domestic service, which runs through Kent into London. On the same day, Prime Minister Gordon Brown would promise to invest £20 billion in railway infrastructure in the coming years. The first Javelin train was named after double Olympic gold medalist Dame Kelly Holmes.

14th December, 2009

Gorilla tactics. A man dressed as a gorilla demonstrates outside the House of Commons in London, urging MPs to do all they can to ensure that Cadbury, the British confectioner, remains independent in the light of a take-over bid mounted by US food giant Kraft. It would be to no avail, however, and the American company would assume control in early February 2010.
16th December, 2009

Rockin' all over the world. Rick Parfitt (L) and Francis Rossi
of Status Quo, who were crowned Britain's hardest working
band after notching up more major concerts in 2009 than
any other group. They had played to over 250,000 fans in 27
different arenas. Both would be awarded OBE's in 2010.
28th December, 2009

The Publishers gratefully acknowledge Press Association Images, from whose extensive archives the photographs in this book have been selected. Personal copies of the photographs in this book, and many others, may be ordered online at www.prints.paphotos.com

For more information, please contact:

Ammonite Press
AE Publications Ltd, 166 High Street, Lewes, East Sussex, BN7 1XU, United Kingdom
Tel: +44 (0)1273 488006 Fax: +44 (0)1273 472418
www.ammonitepress.com